My *B*allet *Book*

My Ballet Book

Lynette Silver in consultation with Kay Smith

GARY ALLEN

First published in 1992
Prepared by Sally Milner Publishing Pty Ltd
for Gary Allen Pty Ltd
9 Cooper Street
Smithfield NSW 2164 Australia

© Lynette Silver, 1992

Production by Sylvana Scannapiego,
Island Graphics
Design by Wing Ping Tong
Cover and book illustrations by Penny Walton
Typeset in Australia by Asset Typesetting Pty Ltd
Printed in Australia by Impact Printing (Vic) Pty Ltd

National Library of Australia
Cataloguing-in-Publication data:

Silver, Lynette Ramsay, 1945–
    My ballet book.

    ISBN 1 875169 15 6.

    1. Ballet dancing – Juvenile literature. I. Smith, Kay.
    II. Title.

792.802

Contents

How Ballet Began

Men and women have danced for thousands of years, even as far back as the time of the early cave dwellers. Ancient cave paintings and other relics show us that dance played an important role in the everyday life of the people as well as in sacred ceremonies. Dancers decorated their bodies with clay, paint, beads, feathers or flowers and frequently wore ornate and elaborate costumes. They used a mixture of mime and dance to give thanks to their gods for a good harvest or a successful hunt, to ask for good fortune, to celebrate a wedding or birth, or perhaps to rejoice in winning a war against a fierce enemy. Some of these age-old dance patterns have survived to the present day and are still performed to the accompaniment of musical instruments that range from simple rhythm sticks to drums, from reed-like flutes to throbbing didgeridoos.

As time passed, cultures became more civilised. People began to dance for pleasure, performing a wide variety of dances, some of which have altered very little over hundreds of years. The very formal and stately dances were

1

seen only in the royal courts or the houses of the rich. On the other hand, the energetic and lively jigs of the country folk were enjoyed in the local village squares.

Quite recently, a very special form of dancing, in which dancers performed complicated and graceful steps, came into being. Enjoyed by people throughout the world, this beautiful form of dancing is known as classical ballet.

Ballet began about five hundred years ago in Italy, which in those days was not one country but was made up of many little kingdoms or states, each with its own ruler. To impress visitors from neighbouring kingdoms, Italian rulers loved to show off by entertaining their guests with lavish mime, music and dance spectacles called *balleti*, which is from the Italian word "to dance". In those days the *balleti* were always performed by courtiers (noblemen belonging to the court), who disguised themselves with wigs and masks so they could take the women's parts as well as those of the men.

When a powerful and influential Italian noblewoman named Catherine de Medici married into the French royal family in 1533, she took her favourite dancers with her to her new home and so the *balleti* came to France. Called *ballet* by the French, this form of dancing became very popular at the royal court. Indeed ballet became such a successful court entertainment that during the reign

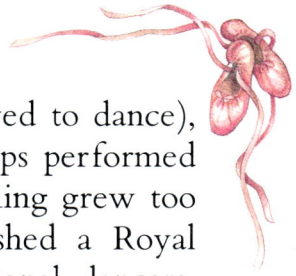

of King Louis XIV (who simply loved to dance), special words were given to the steps performed by the dancers. In 1661, when the King grew too fat to dance any more, he established a Royal Dancing Academy to train professional dancers. The Academy devised the five basic positions of the feet on which all ballet is based. It was at this stage that ballet moved out of the court and into the theatre. Shortly afterwards, ladies also began to dance in the ballet and very soon male dancers had to give up wigs and their female roles.

During the next three hundred years, ballet dancing spread to many countries. Although the dancers' clothing changed and new dancing styles were introduced, ballet kept the words which the French had given to the various steps in 1661. These words are still used throughout the world, making ballet a truly international form of dance.

Classical ballet is more popular today than it has ever been. Each year millions of people flock to theatres all over the world to enjoy the wonderful experience of a live ballet performance and to listen to the magnificent music which famous composers have written especially for the ballet. No matter which country you visit, in most big cities you will find a ballet company performing well-known classical ballets. You will also find, in large cities and small towns, ballet

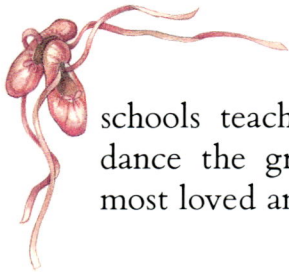

schools teaching young people like you how to dance the graceful steps which make ballet the most loved and admired of all the dance forms.

Choosing Your Ballet School

Most girls want to learn ballet at some time or other. If this is something that you would like to do, you will find that in most cities, towns and suburbs there will be at least one reputable ballet school teaching what is known as classical ballet.

In some countries the same method is taught almost everywhere. In others, ballet schools use methods from all over the world, such as those offered by the Royal Academy of Dance (RAD), the British Ballet Organisation (BBO), Cecchetti and the Russian method. However, the steps and movements of classical ballet are basically the same in all methods of teaching.

Provided you and your parents are prepared to visit schools and ask questions, you should be able to find a school, a teacher and a method which suits you best. If you are not sure whether you really want to learn ballet, ask the school if you can come to watch and perhaps even join in a class, so that you can see what it is like.

After you have been learning ballet for a while, you will know how much time you are

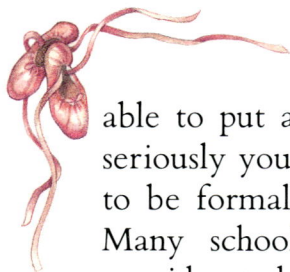

able to put aside for lessons each week and how seriously you wish to study it. Not all pupils have to be formally examined at the end of the year. Many schools offer an annual assessment and provide students with a certificate showing that they have completed a year of classical ballet, which allows them to move up to the next level.

For those who wish to attend class two or three times a week and study ballet seriously, formal examinations at the end of the year are a necessary part of the course. Depending on your local Department of Education or School Board, you might find that you can take classical ballet as part of your final secondary school examination course.

Getting Ready for Your First Lesson

Clothing

Once you have made up your mind that you really want to learn ballet and have picked out the school you wish to attend, you will have the exciting task of buying your very first ballet clothes. In your eagerness to get started, don't forget that you should *not* go shopping until *after* you have actually enrolled at your ballet school.

When you meet your teacher, she will tell you what to buy and will recommend the shops that will be able to supply you with the correct clothing for your lessons. Ballet schools have individual outfits in the same way that ordinary schools have their own special uniforms. Remember that although short, fluffy tulle tutus and longer romantic tutus are pretty (and that every girl who learns ballet dreams of wearing them), tutus are only worn for performances. Not even professional ballerinas wear proper tutus to class. They appear on stage in their beautiful classical ballet costumes, but for practice they wear clothes very similar to those chosen by your teacher for your lessons.

Romantic tutu   Tutu

Leotard and tights

For most ballet classes, students wear a leotard —
a close-fitting body suit that is a little like a
swimsuit. The leotard owes its name to the outfit
worn by the famous French trapeze artist Jules
Leotard. Leotards can be short-sleeved or
sleeveless, can have round or V necks, and can
be any colour. Your teacher will tell you what
design and what colour she wants you to wear.
However, they must always be close fitting and
never fussy, so that your teacher can see clearly
whether the line of your body is correct. Although
some schools like pupils to wear socks, leotards
are often worn over pale pink tights. Some teachers

Pupil wearing a leotard and gauze skirt

might also ask you to wear a short, circular see-through skirt in the same shade as your leotard. This is put on after the leotard and fastens very simply around the waist.

Ballet shoes

We now come to the most important part of any ballerina's ballet wardrobe — the ballet shoe.

There are two types of ballet shoes — a soft shoe and a much harder *pointe* shoe, which has a blocked toe and is specially designed to support the ballet dancer's foot when she is old enough, and experienced enough, to go up on her toes. Going on to your toes, which is called *en pointe*, looks very elegant but not even the world's greatest ballerinas were allowed to do this until

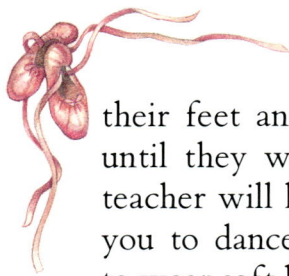

their feet and bones had developed properly and until they were quite experienced dancers. Your teacher will know when the time is right to allow you to dance *en pointe*; until then, you will need to wear soft ballet shoes with flexible leather soles.

Ballet shoes for girls are always coloured pink (to tone with their tights) and are made of soft leather, satin or canvas. It is very important to buy your shoes from a reputable store and to have them fitted properly, otherwise you will have problems with your feet and will not be able to dance properly. Since the shoes are handmade, they are quite expensive and you must take good care of them. Only wear them during your ballet class or while you are practising at home, so that they will last as long as possible.

When you buy your ballet shoes, you will find that they do not have any ribbons or elastic attached. These have to be purchased separately. Your teacher will tell you whether to buy elastic or ribbons, which will then need to be sewn into place very carefully. For each shoe you will need about one metre of one centimetre wide, pink satin ribbon, or about ten centimetres of pink, one centimetre wide elastic.

Before the elastic or ribbons are attached, make sure that the shoe fits your foot snugly by pulling the ends of the drawstring at the front of the shoe. When the shoe feels comfortable, tie the

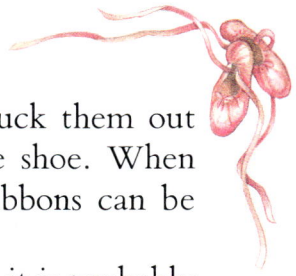

ends of the drawstring firmly and tuck them out of sight under the front edge of the shoe. When this has been done, the elastic or ribbons can be sewn into place.

Unless you are experienced, it is probably a good idea to ask an adult to do this sewing for you, since the ends of the elastic or ribbon must be stitched on in the correct position very firmly and neatly, with no ragged ends showing. You must

Sewing on the ribbons

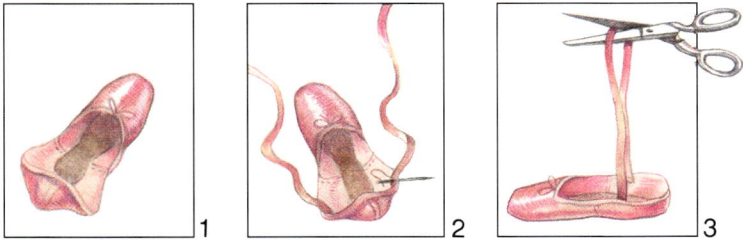

1 To find out where to sew the ribbons, fold the heel forward along the sole.

2 On the fold line, carefully centre the ends of the ribbon on the *inside* of the shoe. Sew the ends firmly into place and then top-sew the ribbon where it meets the edge of the shoe.

3 Pull the loop of the ribbon tight and cut it in the middle, so that you will have two ribbons the same length. The lengths can always be adjusted later to suit the individual foot.
Note: If using elastic, sew the ends in the same position as the ribbons, making sure that the elastic strap fits snugly across the instep.

also remember not to make a knot in the end of the sewing thread as this might rub against the side of your foot and be very uncomfortable. To find out where to sew the elastic or ribbons, look at the illustrations below.

If you have ribbons on your shoes, you must learn how to tie them correctly. To do this, your foot should be flat on the floor (otherwise the ribbons will either be too tight or too loose

Tying the ribbons

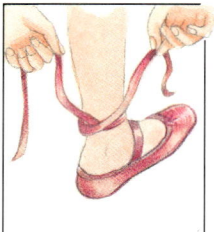

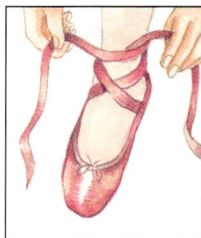

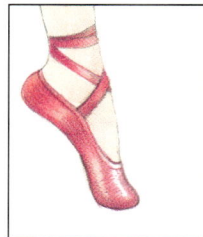

1 Place your foot flat on the floor. Cross the ribbons at the front of your ankle.

2 Now cross the ribbons behind your ankle, and bring them around to the front again.

3 Once again, cross the ribbons at the front of your ankle, just above the first cross-over.

4 Knot the ribbons twice on the inside of your ankle with a flat knot. Tuck the ends, and drawstring, in neatly.

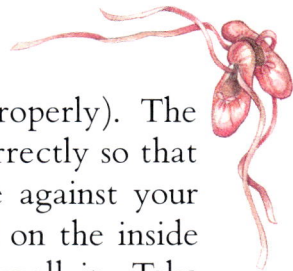

and will not support your ankle properly). The pictures show you how to do this correctly so that the ribbons lie flat and comfortable against your ankle. The knot should then be tied on the inside of your ankle and the ends tucked well in. Take special care not to knot the ribbons at the *back* of your ankle where there is an important, but easily bruised, tendon called the Achilles tendon.

Other clothing

While leotard, tights and ballet shoes are usually the only special clothes worn during the actual lesson, you might find that you need other clothes to keep you warm before class begins. There are generally no special rules about what should be worn, but most pupils choose a long-sleeved cross-over top and perhaps leg-warmers or leggings, which are rather like woolly tights without any feet. The tops and leggings are useful as they not only keep you warm but can also be removed quickly and easily when the lesson is about to begin.

Jewellery

One thing that should not be worn in class is jewellery — not even a watch. Jewellery, especially the glittery or dangling kind, is very distracting; should you unexpectedly collide with another dancer, it can get caught and cause injuries. If you

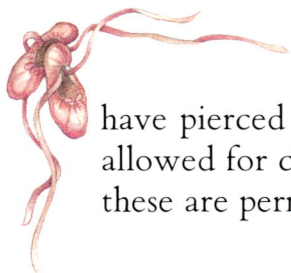

have pierced ears, simple stud earrings are usually allowed for class, but you might find that not even these are permitted for examinations.

Hair

Hair is a most important part of a ballet dancer's grooming and discipline. Except for special character dances which might need pigtails or some other special hairdo, all ballet dancers wear their hair off their faces and their necks. This is necessary to give a good line, to keep you cool, to stop your hair from flicking into your eyes and irritating them, and to allow you to see properly, no matter how energetic the movement. If you have very long hair, pulling it back will also stop it flopping about and upsetting your balance.

There are quite a few suitable styles, especially if you have medium length or long hair.

Classic hairstyle

Braid

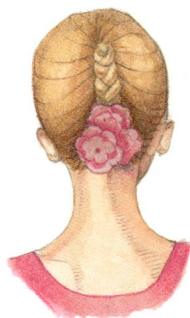

Bun

Hairstyles that suit longer hair are buns, plaits wound across the top of your head, or any type of braiding. Pony tails are no good, as the hair bounces about too much. If you have short hair, it too must be pulled back off your face. Buns need to be pinned into place securely, and a net, the same colour as your hair, placed over it to stop stray bits from creeping out. Depending on your teacher, you might also wear a circlet of flowers, a ribbon or some other hair decoration around your bun. It is important to remember that no matter what hairstyle you choose, it must be neat, unfussy and lie flat on your head.

Make-up

Although make-up is a very important part of the costume in all ballets performed on stage before an audience, it is most unsuitable for class lessons. However, at a special concert or performance you may be allowed to wear lipstick, eye make-up and some blusher if your teacher thinks it is appropriate. Be guided by her — she knows what will look best on the night.

And now, dressed in your ballet outfit, with your hair neatly styled and your jewellery removed, you are ready to go to your very first lesson.

The Ballet Studio

Ballet lessons can be held in special studios, church or school halls, community centres, sports gymnasiums, or indeed any place that provides a spacious and uncarpeted floor area. Although all ballet schools and their studios are different, there are one or two things which you can expect to see, no matter how large or small the school.

When you enter the room you will notice that the floor is quite bare and that there is a smooth wooden handrail attached at about waist height to at least one wall. This is called a *barre* and is used at every lesson, when ballet dancers lightly place one hand on it while practising exercises. Many studios also have large mirrors on the walls so that you can see from your reflection whether you are holding yourself in the correct position. There will be a piano and a pianist, or a tape recorder, to provide the music. If the floor is very slippery, there might also be a shallow box holding *rosin* powder. This is a special powder which dancers use to stop the soles of their ballet shoes sliding about too much.

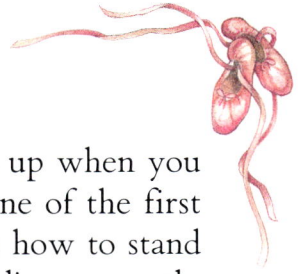

Standing correctly

Although you learned how to stand up when you were not much more than a baby, one of the first things your teacher will show you is how to stand *properly*. A ballet dancer who is standing correctly should always look poised and at ease. If you practise standing correctly as often as you can, you too will look as graceful as the ballet dancer in the picture.

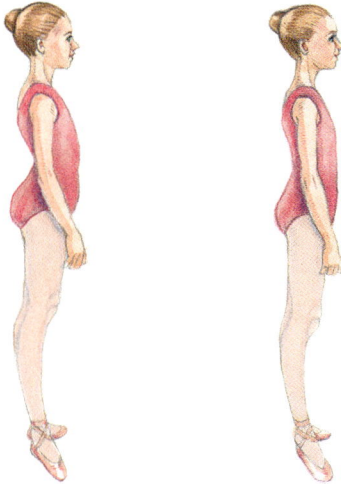

Standing poorly   Standing correctly

Turnout

Your teacher will also explain to you what she means by "turnout". In classical ballet, having a good turnout means the way in which you are

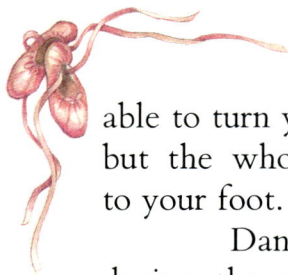

able to turn your legs out, not just from the ankle, but the whole of your leg from your hip joint to your foot.

Dancers first began to turn out their legs during the reign of Louis XIV, when the male dancers at his court wanted to show off their shapely calf muscles and the elegant heels of their shoes. Since many of the ballet steps were especially designed to display these features, a good turnout of the legs was essential.

Because today's ballet dancers perform these very same steps, turnout is just as important now as it was three hundred years ago. Turning out your legs properly also enables you to lift them higher and helps to create a streamlined look. Exercises to strengthen your turnout must be practised constantly, even when you are an accomplished ballet dancer.

The Ballet Lesson

Usually a ballet lesson is split into two parts — *barre* work followed by *centre* work.

Barre work

Exercises at the *barre* are to make your body supple and warm and to strengthen your muscles so that you can perform movements without losing your balance when you move into the centre of the room.

Ballet exercises at the *barre* perform a job rather like the first row of building blocks in a wall. Unless the blocks are strong and correctly placed, the rest of the wall cannot be built without toppling over. Just like the base of a wall, your *barre* work gives you a firm foundation on which to build all your ballet movements.

Centre work

When your teacher is satisfied that you have spent enough time at the *barre*, you will move into the centre of the room for what is known as *centre*

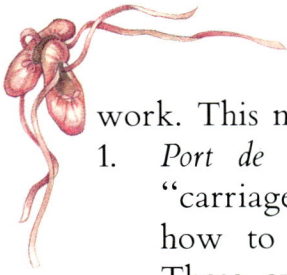

work. This normally is split into several sections:

1. *Port de bras* is the French expression for "carriage of the arms", in which you learn how to make your arm movements flow. These exercises also help you to develop a good line by coordinating the movements of your head, body and arms. All *port de bras* movements should flow smoothly from one pose to the next to give good continuity. They should never be jerky or hurried.

2. Some of the exercises which you practised at the *barre* will also be done in *centre* work.

3. *Pirouettes* —when turns or spins on one leg are practised.

4. *Adage* (from the Italian words *ad agio* meaning "at ease") — slow movements to help you control your balance and develop poise.

5. *Allegro* (an Italian musical term meaning "quick and lively") — quicker movements, such as turns and jumps (*petit allegro*), followed by larger leaps called *grand allegro*.

After *centre* work exercises comes the favourite part of the lesson, when pupils put the steps they have been learning into dance. Depending on the method of ballet you are learning, during this time you may also learn what is known as *character dancing*. Character dances are folk dances which come from many different countries, and are very

Pupil wearing character skirt
and character shoes

Ballet dancer in
character costume

distinctive. For this type of dance you probably will be asked to pop on a character skirt, which is generally a full skirt (in a colour to tone with your leotard) which has two or three rows of braid sewn around the hem. You may also change from your ballet shoes to special character shoes, which are usually made of black leather with a small heel and a single strap.

Because ballet began in the royal court, where manners were very important, the lesson always ends with the *reverence*, when pupils curtsey to the pianist and to the teacher to show their appreciation. If you have ever attended a ballet you may have noticed that the dancers use this same graceful curtsey at the end of every performance.

Ballet Steps and Movements

Every step in ballet is based on one of seven movements — bending, gliding, turning, stretching, jumping, rising and darting. Because ballet became popular in the French court, the names given to movements, as well as the steps, are always in French. The words generally describe what movement is being done (such as stretching, leaping, sliding, etc.), the direction to move, or the position of the step. Some of the terms which you might need to know are listed below. The words are not hard to pronounce and it will not be long before you are able to remember all the French terms to go with the steps.

Movements

Attitude	A position or pose where you stand on one leg and lift and bend the other leg forward or back.
Arabesque	A position or pose where you balance on one leg and raise the other to the back, extending it as far as possible.
Battement	A beating movement of the leg.
Bras	Arms.

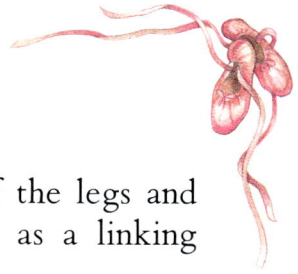

Bras bas	Arms down.
Changement	Changing.
Chassé	A sliding movement of the legs and feet — normally used as a linking step.
Croisé	Crossed.
Demi	Half.
Demi-pointe	Half-point — taking the weight on the ball of the foot.
Développé	An unfolding of the leg and arm into any open position.
Echappé	Escaped.
Enchainement	A linking or chain of steps.
En pointe	On the toes.
Frappé	Struck.
Grand	Big.
Glissade	A glide or slide.
Glissé	Gliding or sliding.
Jambe	Leg.
Jeté	Thrown.
Pas	A step or dance.
Pirouette	To spin or turn on one leg.
Plié	A bending of the knees.
Port de bras	Carriage or movement of the arms.
Petit	Small.
Relevé	Raised — a snatching movement of the feet into a *demi-pointe* position.
Retiré	Withdrawn — a movement where the toe of one shoe is drawn up to

23

the small hollow on the inside of the
knee of the supporting leg.

Sauté   To spring.
Temps lié   A movement to bend, link or join.
Tendu   Stretched.

Directions

A la seconde To the side — second position.
A terre   On the ground.
Derrière   Behind.
Devant   In front.
En arrière   Backwards.
En avant   Forwards.
En bas   Down.
En croix   In the shape of a cross.
En dedans   To the inside — towards the support-
                ing leg.
En dehors   To the outside — away from the
                supporting leg.
En face   Facing the front.
En l'air   In the air.
Rond   Round.

Positions

Première   First.
Seconde   Second.
Troisième   Third.

Quatrième	Fourth.
Cinquième	Fifth.

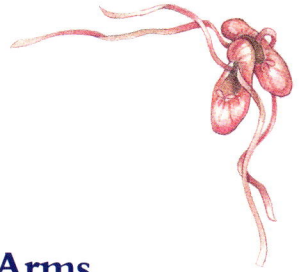

The Positions of the Feet and Arms

After you have been shown how to stand correctly, you will learn the five positions of the feet and the positions of the arms. All ballet movements are based on these very important positions.

First   Second

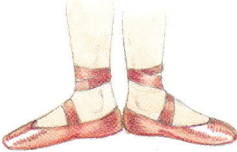

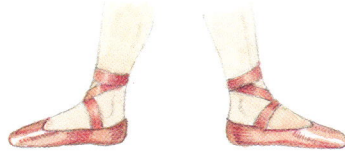

Third   Fourth (opposite first)

Fourth (opposite fifth)   Fifth

Positions of the feet

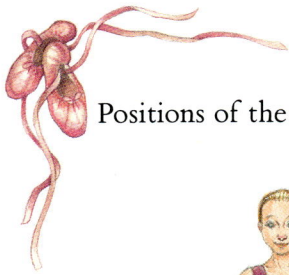

Positions of the arms

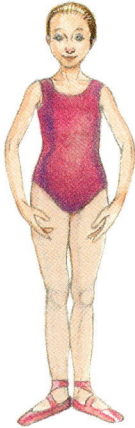

Bra bas

First

Fourth

Fifth

Attitude or open fourth

Second

Third

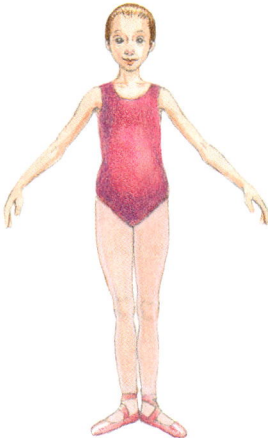

Demi second

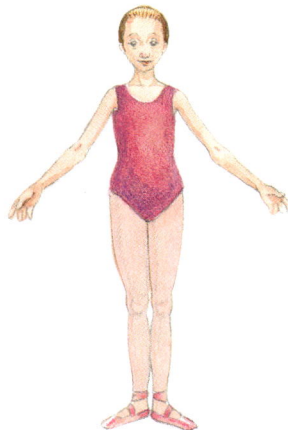

Demi bras

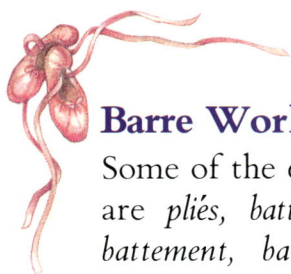

Barre Work

Some of the exercises you will practice at the *barre* are *pliés*, *battements* (such as *grand battement, petit battement, battement glissé* and *battement frappé*), *relevés, retirés, ronds de jambe à terre* and *développés*.

Pliés

A *plié*, from the French word "to bend", is a bending of the knees. Since *pliés* stretch all the

Grand plié in first position

Demi plié in first position

Demi plié in second position

muscles of your legs and are performed in all five positions, they are excellent warming-up exercises. A *plié* can be either a *demi* (half) or *grand* (full). *Pliés* are important as they give flexibility to the knees and help strengthen your turnout.

Battement

The following pictures show just two of the many different forms of *battement*, the French word which describes a beating movement of the leg.

Battement tendu — to perform *battement tendu*, your leg must be fully stretched. This exercise strengthens all your leg muscles.

Battement tendu

29

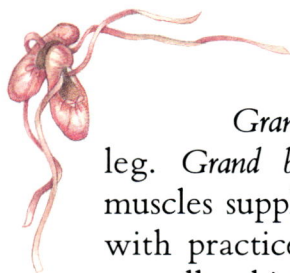

Grand battement — a high throw of the leg. *Grand battement* helps to make your thigh muscles supple and improves your turnout so that, with practice, your leg movements will be light as well as high.

Grand battement

When you have completed *battement* exercises in front, to the side and behind you (*devant, à la seconde* and *derrière*), you will have made a pattern in the shape of a cross. This is called *en croix*. Many exercises besides *battements* are performed *en croix*.

Relevés

Relevés are light, quick movements, which also could be described as snatches, when you rise on to the balls of your feet (*demi-pointe*). Later, when you are ready, you will perform *relevés en pointe* (on your toes). *Relevés* may be performed on one foot with the other leg raised (*en l'air*) in any position, or on both feet, also in any position.

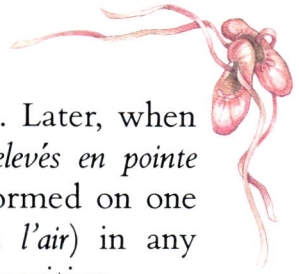

Retiré

In the *retiré* position, the toe of your working leg is drawn up to the small hollow on the inside of the knee of your supporting leg. For a small (*petit*) *retiré*, the toe of your working foot is only raised to ankle height. Practising *retirés* will help strengthen your turnout.

Retiré

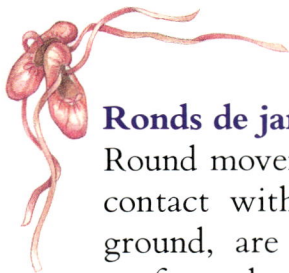

Ronds de jambe à terre

Round movements of the leg, keeping the foot in contact with the ground, with the toe on the ground, are *ronds de jambe à terre*. They can be performed outwards (*en dehors*), when the working leg circles to the back, or inwards (*en dedans*), when the working leg rotates to the front. *Ronds de jambe à terre*, which need a good turnout, are practiced so that your hip joint will rotate your leg freely, without moving the rest of your body. When you have completed the movements that make up *ronds de jambe à terre*, you will have traced out the shape of a semi-circle. The illustrations show *ronds de jambe à terre en dehors*.

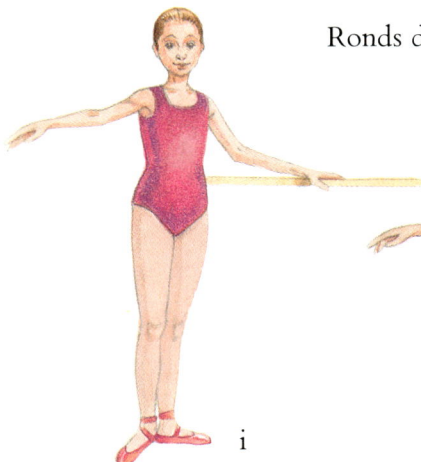

Ronds de jambe à terre en dehors

i

ii

iii

iv

v

Développé

A *développé* is a slow, controlled movement in which you unfold your leg and arm to produce a beautiful line with your body. *Développés*, like

Développé devant

other *barre* exercises, may be performed *en croix* — that is, in front (*devant*), to the side (*à la seconde*) or behind (*derrière*). The illustration shows *développé devant*.

Centre Work

After you have finished your *port de bras* and practised in the centre of the room the exercises you have already performed at the *barre* (such as *pliés* and *battements*), you will usually move on to *pirouettes*, followed by *adage* and *allegro*.

Pirouettes

Pirouette is the French word for a whirl or a spin. As *pirouettes* can be performed either slowly (*adage*) or very fast (*allegro*), they really form a section on their own. There are many types of *pirouettes*. Until you gain some experience, you will practise your *pirouettes* at the *barre*. Your first *pirouettes* will be *demi-pointe* (on the balls of your feet). Later you will learn to *pirouette en pointe*.

Because spinning can make you feel dizzy, ballet dancers have to "spot" when *pirouetting*, so that they do not lose their sense of balance and fall over. You learn to "spot" by looking at a fixed spot or object, which you choose to suit you. You then focus on it for as long as possible while you are turning, before flicking your head around quickly and focusing on it again.

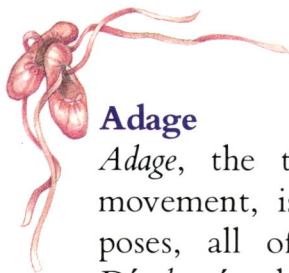

Adage

Adage, the term used to describe slow dance movement, is really a combination of steps and poses, all of which are slow and controlled. *Développé*, which has already been described in the section on *barre* work, is one of these, but there are several others.

Chassé (from the French word meaning "chased"), is a sliding of the legs and feet. *Chassés* are normally used as linking steps.

Temps lié is a connected movement which takes its meaning from the French word "to join" and which teaches you how to transfer your weight from one leg to another. In the early stages, you will perform this with your feet on the ground (*à terre*) but later, when you are more experienced, you will progress to *temps lié en l'air* (in the air), which is more complicated.

Arabesque is probably the most graceful of all the classical poses, as you can see from the illustration. To perform an *arabesque*, you take the weight of your body on one leg, while extending the other fully, and at the same time placing your arms in a position to give the longest line possible from fingers to toes. Line is extremely important in an *arabesque*, which can be *à terre*, when the working foot is on the ground, or *en l'air*, when the working foot is raised.

Arabesque (en l'air)

Attitude is another very graceful pose, in which the weight of your body is taken on one leg, while the other is lifted and bent, either to the back (*attitude derrière*) or the front (*attitude devant*).

Attitude (derrière)

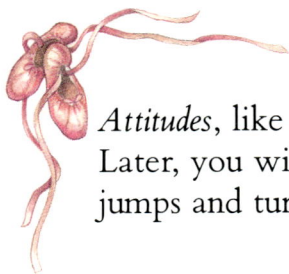

Attitudes, like *arabesques*, are not just beautiful poses. Later, you will learn how to incorporate them into jumps and turns.

Allegro

Because *allegro* is quick and lively, it is usually left until your muscles are well and truly warmed up. Some *allegro* movements, such as the running steps of *pas de bourrée* are small and neat (*petit allegro*) while others, such as leaps or *grands jetés*, are large and energetic (*grand allegro*). The following steps and jumps are just some of those you will learn during the *allegro* part of your ballet lesson.

STEPS

Glissades are gliding steps which enable you to travel sideways by sliding your feet along the floor to the left, right, forwards or backwards. In the beginning, you will perform your *glissades* slowly, but you will soon build up speed so that in time they will become faster and faster. Although *glissades* are quick movements, they must also be smooth.

Pas de bourrée are intricate running steps. They can be used by themselves or to move from one position to another. When you see a dancer move with apparent ease *en pointe* across the stage, using tiny steps that seem to twinkle, she is performing one type of *pas de bourrée*.

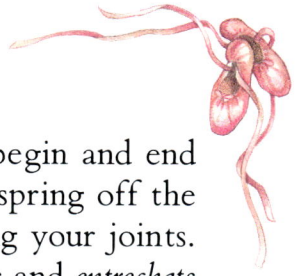

JUMPS

All jumps, whether large or small, begin and end with a *demi-plié*. This enables you to spring off the ground and then land without jarring your joints.

Sautés, soubresauts, changements and entrechats are all jumps where the dancer springs straight into the air with legs fully stretched from a *demi-plié* and returns to a *demi-plié* position. However, each jump has its special differences.

A *sauté* (the French word for "jump") is a very simple jump where the dancer springs into the air with legs fully stretched, from a *demi-plié* and returns to exactly the *same* position. The illustration shows the dancer beginning her *sauté* in first position and ending in that same position.

Sauté in first position

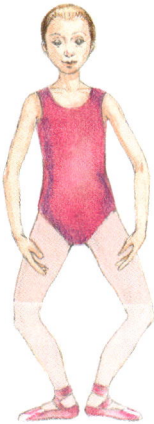

i   ii   iii

A *soubresaut* is a simple *sauté* done in fifth position.

An *échappé sauté* is a little different. In this movement (from the French words meaning "escape" and "jump"), the feet escape from one position to another. For example, the dancer begins with a *demi-plié* in *first* position, springs with legs fully stretched, escaping from that position to finish in *second* position.

In a *changement* (from the French word "to change"), the dancer also springs into the air with legs fully stretched from a *demi-plié* (either third or fifth position). However, she changes the position of her feet during the jump, so that when she lands the foot that was *behind* when she began

Changement

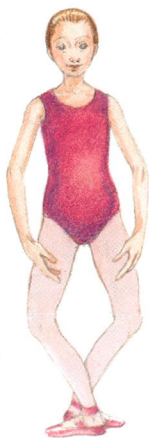

i   ii   iii

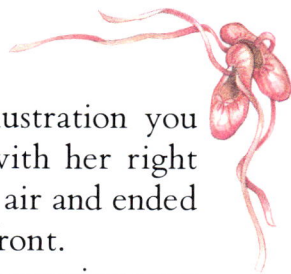

the jump is now in *front*. In the illustration you will notice that the dancer began with her right foot in front, changed position in the air and ended the movement with her left foot in front.

An *entrechat* is a "beating" or crossing over of the feet in the air. To perform an *entrechat*, you jump straight into the air from a *demi-plié* and then, depending on the type of *entrechat*, you cross and recross your feet a number of times before landing. *Entrechats* are very suited to athletic male dancers. The Russian dancer Nijinsky is said to have crossed and uncrossed his feet in the air six times before landing.

Jetés, assemblés and *pas de chat* are also jumps, but unlike *sautés, soubresauts* and *changements*, you spring from one leg and land on the other.

In a *jeté* (from the French work meaning "thrown") the working leg is swished out from the supporting leg. When practising *jeté devant* and *jeté derrière* (in front and behind), care has to be taken that the body does not travel sideways but lands in the same spot. A *jeté* can be either small (*petit*) or large (*grand*).

In an *assemblé* the feet, which have been separated during the jump, join together (or assemble) in the air before landing in a *demi-plié*.

Pas de chat, which means "step of a cat", is fun to do. It is really a series of steps in the *retiré* and *pirouette* positions which are alternated to

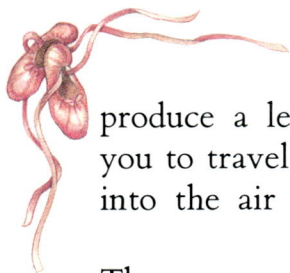

produce a leaping movement. *Pas de chat* allows you to travel sideways, rather like a cat springing into the air with all four paws off the ground.

The steps and movements described or illustrated in this book are, of course, only a few of the many that you will learn while your are studying ballet. As you become more experienced, you will be able to perform the hundreds of variations to the basic steps which make classical ballet such a rewarding and exciting experience.

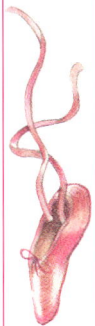

Examinations

Just as regular school subjects have different examinations, so each different ballet method has its own examination system. At each level, pupils of a certain age or ability are expected to be able to perform properly the movements and steps they have been learning in class. If you decide to take examinations, your teacher will tell you well in advance what will be examined and will give you plenty of practice so that when the time comes you will be ready for the examiner.

Examiners are specially chosen people who are very experienced in the ballet method you are studying. Their task is to watch you very carefully as you go through your ballet exercises and dances. Because examiners see many pupils dancing at many different schools, they are able to decide whether you are dancing well enough to move up to the next grade. Examiners can either come out to your ballet school or ask you to travel to an examination centre.

As this will be a very special occasion, you must look your best. Take the time to make sure that your outfit is spotless, that your hair is

clean and neat and that your shoes are correctly tied with no untidy ribbon ends flapping about. If your ballet method prefers you to wear special clothes or shoes to the examination, your teacher will tell you exactly what you need and will give you plenty of notice. Some time after your exam, you will be given a report and a certificate, signed by your examiner.

Assessments

Students who do not wish to be formally examined may like to take advantage of an individual assessment, which many ballet schools offer as an alternative to examinations. Like the examiner, the person making the assessment will be someone with an excellent knowledge of ballet. Students who have been assessed will also receive a report and certificate.

Eisteddfods

Eisteddfod is a Welsh word which describes a special competition for artists such as singers, dancers, musicians and actors. These are usually held each year in most large centres. Although only a small number of pupils learning ballet will want to enter eisteddfods, those who do so will find it quite an experience. Eisteddfods not only provide ballet dancers with an opportunity to perform in front of an audience, but they also give each contestant an idea of how she measures up against others in the same age group.

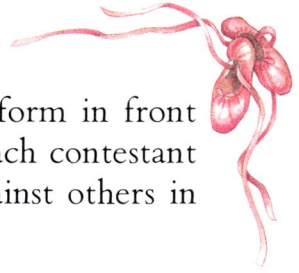

Dance Quality and the Dancer

Unlike the movements and terms described in this book, dance quality is something that can not adequately be put into words, nor completely captured by even the most sophisticated camera or most talented painter. Despite this, dance quality *is* instantly recognisable.

Dance quality is a combination of technical excellence, a beautiful line, flowing movements, artistic interpretation, the ability to be as one with the music, and an indefinable quality that comes from within the dancer. It is this last quality that makes excellent dancers exceptional.

However, all these attributes count for nothing if dancers fail to remember that they are not dancing for themselves, but for their audience. If they can dance so that the audience enjoys their performance to the utmost, then they will be well on the way to becoming great *artistes*. It is this ability to give individual pleasure, every time they perform, that makes ballet dancers not merely exceptional but truly great.

Handy Tips for Budding Ballet Dancers

- Pink ballet shoes can be spruced up with an application of pink calamine lotion. Calamine lotion, which is quite powdery when it dries, is also very good for reducing the shine on new satin ballet shoes before a performance. The matte finish allows the shoes to blend in with the matte surface of the tights, giving an uninterrupted line from toe to hip.

- Marks on leather ballet shoes (especially marks made by shoe polish or ball-point pen) can usually be removed by applying hair spray, eucalyptus oil, methylated spirits or tea-tree oil and then rubbing lightly with a soft rag.

- Scoring the leather on the soles of ballet shoes with a pair of pointed scissors in a criss-cross pattern will help prevent them from being too slippery.

- Colourless nail polish painted on the ends of ballet shoe ribbons will stop them fraying. Colourless polish is also handy for stopping ladders from running in ballet tights.

- Spraying the knot on the ballet shoe ribbons with hair spray will help stop the ends working loose — something that must not happen during a performance or examination.
- Satin *pointe* shoes will last much longer if the toes are darned. Fine, pink crochet-cotton is best for this as it is much stronger than ordinary sewing thread.
- Hair decorations for concerts and performances need not be expensive. With a little imagination you can turn pipe cleaners, Christmas decorations, items from haberdashery counters, household odds and ends, recycled sequins, glittery buttons and old jewellery into very attractive hair ornaments.

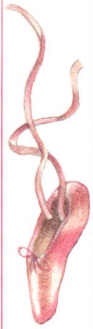

My Ballet Diary

Whenever you see a ballet, whether it is performed on stage, or is screened on television or at the cinema, try to make a record of the name of the ballet and the date in this diary. You could also add the name of the company, the soloists, what you thought of the performance, and perhaps a small sketch or a picture cut from the programme.

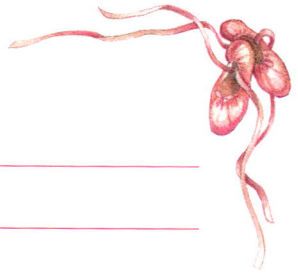

51

My Own
Special Achievements

Because there are so many special events that take place while you are learning ballet, you might like to keep a record of them here. Perhaps you could include the details of your first lesson, the assessments or exams you have passed, a note or two about eisteddfods and concerts in which you have taken part, the date you wore your first tutu or *pointe* shoes, or anything else that happened that was special for you.

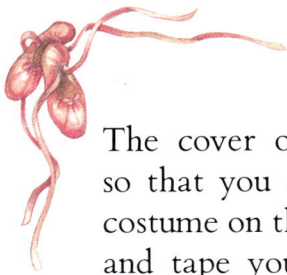

The cover of *My Ballet Book* has been designed so that you can put a photo of yourself in ballet costume on the cover. To do this, remove the jacket and tape your photo over the picture that is on the cover, then put the jacket back in place. You will now be in the frame on the front of the book.